BASIS FOR BUSINESS **C1**
WORKBOOK

MINDY EHRHART KRULL

ADVISER
PAUL KAVANAGH, BREMEN

Basis for Business C1
Workbook

Im Auftrag des Verlages erarbeitet von	Mindy Ehrhart Krull, Dresden
Beratende Mitarbeit	Paul Kavanagh, Bremen
Redaktion	Stephanie Hempel, München
Redaktionelle Mitarbeit	Rebecca Banks
Projektkoordination	Anna Batrla
Projektleitung	Andreas Goebel
Umschlaggestaltung	hawemannundmosch, konzeption und gestaltung, Berlin
Layout und technische Umsetzung	Sabine Theuring, Berlin
Cover	iStockphoto, Yuri

Bildquellen
S. 7 © iStockphoto, quavondo; S. 10 © Sergey Nivens/fotolia; S. 17 © Rido/fotolia;
S. 24 © arekmalang/fotolia; S. 36 © goodluz/fotolia; S. 46 © Studioloco/Shutterstock

Weitere Kursmaterialien
Coursebook mit Audio-CD und Phrasebook   ISBN 978-3-06-521020-1
Teaching Guide (online)   ISBN 978-3-06-520474-3

www.cornelsen.de

1. Auflage, 2. Druck 2021

© 2014 Cornelsen Schulverlag GmbH, Berlin
© 2021 Cornelsen Verlag GmbH, Berlin

Das Werk und seine Teile sind urheberrechtlich geschützt.
Jede Nutzung in anderen als den gesetzlich zugelassenen Fällen bedarf der
vorherigen schriftlichen Einwilligung des Verlages.
Hinweis zu §§ 60 a, 60 b UrhG: Weder das Werk noch seine Teile dürfen ohne eine
solche Einwilligung an Schulen oder in Unterrichts- und Lehrmedien (§ 60 b Abs. 3 UrhG)
vervielfältigt, insbesondere kopiert oder eingescannt, verbreitet oder in ein Netzwerk
eingestellt oder sonst öffentlich zugänglich gemacht oder wiedergegeben werden.
Dies gilt auch für Intranets von Schulen.

Druck: H. Heenemann, Berlin

ISBN 978-3-06-521021-8

PEFC zertifiziert
Dieses Produkt stammt aus nachhaltig bewirtschafteten Wäldern und kontrollierten Quellen.
www.pefc.de

Table of contents

Unit			Page
1	Working together	• talk about jobs and industries • write your profile • respond to different communication styles • discuss on-the-job training	5
2	Business processes	• describe processes and core operations • review and solve problems with processes • write a report • read recommendations from business practice	11
3	Project management	• discuss schedules and clarify next steps • request and examine a Proposal for Services • read about Scrum and knowledge management	17
4	International teams	• communicate about operations and logistics • practise teleconferencing language • practise dealing with conflict • examine cultural differences	24
5	Sustainable business	• explore sustainability • review financial performance • pitch financial services • practise business storytelling and reporting	30
6	Managing people	• debate the pros and cons of workplace conditions • recount an HR incident • practise giving feedback • discuss assessment methods	36
7	Meeting demand	• contrast marketing practices • practise networking • discuss intellectual property issues • handle formal correspondence • discuss brands and social marketing	43
8	Public relations	• discuss codes of business conduct • handle difficult questions • explore corporate social responsibility • write a press release • deal with social media for PR	48
	Progress checks		54
	Answer key (exercises and progress checks)		58
	Transcripts		68

Preface

Das **Basis for Business C1** Workbook hilft Ihnen, Ihre Englischkenntnisse selbstständig zu erweitern. Durch das handliche Pocket-Format kann Sie das Workbook überall begleiten: Auf dem Weg zur Arbeit, auf Geschäftsreisen, in einer Kaffeepause oder am Schreibtisch.

Die abwechslungsreichen Übungen im Workbook erweitern und vertiefen die im Kursbuch **Basis for Business C1** behandelten Themen und Strukturen. Das Workbook kann dabei sowohl zum Selbststudium zu Hause als auch im Unterricht verwendet werden.

Das **Basis for Business C1** Workbook ist in acht Units unterteilt, die auf das Kursbuch abgestimmt sind. Sie enthalten:
- Übungen zu den wichtigsten Grammatikstrukturen und zum Wortschatz
- Over to you-Übungen, um das Gelernte zu personalisieren
- sprachliche Tipps und Did you know?-Kästen mit ergänzenden Informationen zum Thema der Unit
- 2 Progress checks zur Selbsteinschätzung und Überprüfung der Lernfortschritte
- Hörverständnisübungen in jeder Unit. Die Audio-Aufnahmen für dieses Workbook finden Sie auf der dem Kursbuch beiliegenden CD (ISBN 978-3-06-521020-1).
- vollständige Transkripte und Lösungen (im Anhang)

Wir wünschen Ihnen mit dem **Basis for Business C1** Workbook viel Spaß und Erfolg!

Working together 1

Unit checklist
- talk about jobs and industries
- write your profile
- respond to different communication styles
- discuss on-the-job training

1 In a similar chart, write a list of your past activities or accomplishments (simple past) and your current tasks or cumulative experience (present perfect [continuous]). In a second step, you could add these statements to the profile you wrote for exercise 7 on page 11 of the coursebook.

Experience	
Simple past	Present perfect (continuous)
I completed my MBA last year.	I've led the department for five years.
In May I attended the conference.	I've been working on the Reynolds project since 2012.
…	…

2 Use the present perfect or present perfect continuous to complete the statements. For two gaps, both can be correct.

1. A: It's already 11. . . . . you . . . . (process) the data?
   B: No, not yet, but we . . . . (work) on it all morning.

2. A: He . . . . (work) in the department since 2012. I think he was transferred from R&D?
   B: Yes, that's right.

3. A: We . . . . (conduct) two proof of efficacy trials since March.
   B: That's great. What did the results show?

4. A: I could really use a break. I . . . . (negotiate) with suppliers for the past three days. All these figures and calculations are running through my head! So far I . . . . only . . . . (close) three deals.
   B: How about going out for a coffee?

5. A: . . . . you . . . . (draft) the proposal?
   B: Yes – actually, I sent it to you on Tuesday and . . . . (wait) for your approval.

Unit **1** Working together 5

3 The words *actual* and *actually* are often used in English. Read transcript 5 on page 132 of the coursebook and find four examples.
Then explain their function.

1 ....
....
2 ....
....
3 ....
....
4 ....
....

4 Match the words to their definitions.
Then write one or two sentences that use at least three of the words.

1	to shadow	a	time away from one's job to care for children
2	to pursue	b	a difficulty or potential problem with meeting the requirements, often official requirements
3	to reboot		
4	parental leave	c	to closely watch how someone works and what he or she does in order to learn more about a job
5	red tape	d	to start again
6	compliance issue	e	rules, regulations, or other official requirements that must be met
		f	to try to achieve

....
....
....
....

> **Did you know?**
>
> Most English-speaking countries do not have a parental leave policy that is comparable to those found in Germany, Austria and Switzerland.

....
....
....

5 Listen to track 7 of the coursebook and read the transcript on pages 133/134 of the coursebook. Identify the phrases or sentences that the speakers use to fulfill different purposes during the meeting. At least two answers are possible for each category.

Questions that check information during introductions	Phrases or sentences that put forward ideas or requests
....	....
....	....
....	....
....	....
....	....
....	....
Phrases or sentences that express empathy or interest	Statements that express knowledge about someone's experience
....	....
....	....
....	....
....	....
....	....
....	....

Tip The phrase *I was wondering* is used in English to begin a polite request, whereas *I wonder* is used more in the sense of *I ask myself*.
I was wondering if we could meet next week.
I wonder what time they will arrive.

Unit **1** Working together

6 In English, the verb *manage* and the phrasal verb *managed to* + infinitive have different meanings.
Match the definition to the correct example.

1	We managed to get products onto the shelves in record time.	a		to be in charge of
2	I managed two full-time employees and three part-time employees in my last job.	b		to be successful in doing something even though it was difficult

Now complete the sentences with the correct word(s) in the box.

> managed (3x) •
> managed to win •
> managed to move •
> managed to reach

1 The negotiations were long and frustrating, but we .... a good deal.

2 We .... the state contract despite the amount of red tape.

3 He .... the project for three years before becoming the department head. Would you believe that during that time he also .... the research department into a new facility?

4 They .... the company from the time it was founded up to when the merger took place.

5 She .... a very heavy workload while she worked here. She was responsible for running the junior executive programme as well as for recruiting new talent at universities throughout Europe.

7 Listen to the audio and identify the four requests that Anna makes. Effective professional communication ideally falls somewhere between Anna's "driver" style and Azra's "amiable" style. Adapt Anna's questions or requests to make them less forceful; then read the transcript on page 67 and adapt Azra's responses so they are less tentative. Several answers are possible.

Anna

1 ....
2 ....
3 I think two days would be best. ....
4 ....

Azra

1 If that's feasible, of course. ....
2 ....
3 ....
4 ....

8 Think about the last time you were in a situation in which you did not understand something that was just explained to you by a foreign business partner. List what you could say to admit you don't understand and ask for the information again.

Thank you for your explanation, but I'm afraid some of the details are a little unclear to me. Would you mind going through it step by step?

9 Find a training course, conference, or programme that is applicable to your job and which you would like to attend. Use at least five words, phrases or concepts mentioned in the text on page 15 of the coursebook or elsewhere in the unit to write an email (or letter) to your supervisor or HR department to request permission. Keep in mind what you learned in the unit about communication styles.

over to you

10 Complete the phrasal verbs from the unit with the correct preposition. In some cases more than one answer is possible. Then add an object to form a collocation or possible phrase.

in • on (4x) • to (2x) • with (3x)

1 to take part .in......

  to take part in a programme, a meeting, a conference, a negotiation, a trial

2 to focus ....

  ....

3 to react ....

  ....

4 to adapt ....

  ....

5 to brief (someone) ....

  ....

6 to negotiate ....

  ....

7 to come .... board

  ....

10 Unit **1** Working together

Business processes 2

Unit checklist
- describe processes and core operations
- review and solve problems with processes
- write a report
- read recommendations from business practice

1 Complete the chart to create word families. Then identify which words might be suitable for you to use to talk about processes in your job or at your company.

Noun	Verb	Adjective (past participle)
validation		
	to confirm	
		notified
	to remit	
shipment		

2 *Effect* and *affect* are often confused in English, also among native speakers. Complete the sentences, then make a note of the differences. Pay close attention to the parts of speech and meanings.

1 We're sorry he's retiring. He always used his strong leadership skills to .... positive changes in the company.

....

2 Hundreds of people in our town are employed by the plant, so the plans to move production overseas will definitely .... the local community.

....

3 We've adapted our processes for the online marketplace, but we haven't seen any positive .... on revenue.

....

3 Melanie Harper was part of a work shadowing programme at her university. In a brief memo to her adviser, Ms Thomas, she must outline a process she learned about while observing the PR department of an SME. Read her narrative explanation and transform it into a memo, converting sentences that could be changed into passive voice as appropriate. It might also be possible to combine some sentences.

> "Press release process: First, members of the department talk with their colleagues in order to gather the information needed for the press release. Then they write a draft of the press release. At least one press officer reads it and requests changes. The members of the department make the requested changes and give the revision to the senior press officer for approval.
> After the senior press officer has approved the revision, the members of the department send it to the department concerned to ensure that all details are accurate. This step is especially important when the news deals with a technical subject. Once they correct any details, they prepare a final draft to distribute to the media. If the news involves another company, at this point they obtain approval from that company. As soon as they receive approval, they post the news to the intranet. Most of the company's employees get an automatic notice when a new press release has been posted, so the PR department usually doesn't need to take any further steps to notify people internally. Finally, they distribute the press release to the media. Once they distribute the press release, they follow up with their media contacts immediately to try to get good coverage in key media outlets."

4 Match the synonyms. Then choose four words and write a short description that includes them.

1	at first	a		nonetheless
2	in spite of that	b		consequently
3	although	c		even though
4	as a result	d		initially

....
....
....
....
....

Tip *First* and *at first* are not interchangeable. *First* is used for the order in which something is done, whereas *at first* is used to signal a contrast between an initial and subsequent action or belief.
First we attended the opening meeting, and then we attended a session on increasing efficiency in processes.
At first we didn't think it was possible to adapt our order process for tablet computers, but then we brought a consultant on board who assured us it was possible.

5 Look at the short report on page 23 of the coursebook. Under each heading, describe the function of that paragraph. Several answers are possible. Then note which tense is used in each section.

Introduction: ....
....

Description: ....
....

Conclusion: ....
....

Recommendations: ....
....

6 Without looking at your coursebook, look at sentences a and b and identify which recommendation is formal (f) and which is less formal (lf).
Then, using the recommendations as a model, write your own recommendations in response to the scenarios.

a If I were you, I'd notify them immediately.
b I advise that you contact them immediately.

1 A colleague talks with you about a recent negotiation.
   A: It's too bad that we couldn't close the deal. We were hoping they would become a key client.
   B: What happened?
   A: Towards the end of the negotiation, there was a misunderstanding about the contract terms.

   B: ....
   ....

2 You are the HR manager and a department head asks you for some suggestions on how to handle an internal conflict.
   A: Thanks very much for meeting with me. Two members of my department seem to be having difficulty working together.
   B: What seems to be the trouble?
   A: Well, it first began with coldness toward each other during meetings, but they were still able to work on the same team. At first I thought the issue would just resolve itself, but now I see that's not going to happen. The situation is causing us to run behind schedule on our projects.
   B: Have you tried talking to them?

A: Yes, separately. Each of them denies that there's any kind of problem.

B: ....

3 You run into a potential customer at a trade fair, and she talks to you about a recent problem she had when placing an order with your company.
   A: We submitted the order online, but never received a confirmation.
   B: Hmm. I work in logistics, so that's not my department, but could you tell me what you did after that?
   A: Well, we sent an email, but never got a response, which was extremely unfortunate because we were hoping that your company would become our new supplier.
   B: I'm afraid I don't know who would be the right contact person in customer service in this case. Let me take your name and forward it on to sales.

   But, in the meantime ....

4 You work as a business consultant and are meeting with a client regarding the future growth of her company. She currently has about 15 full-time employees.
   A: Well, my revenues have grown by about 20 percent for the past four years. Honestly, I don't see how they will increase any further without a dramatic step on my part. Do you see any possibility for my business to grow with minimal financial risk while better utilizing my current staff? I'm uncomfortable making a large financial investment at the moment – but my employees are just fantastic.
   B: That's an excellent question. ....

7 Match the synonyms in the box to the verbs from track 9. Then find a collocation that uses each verb or write in the collocations from the transcript on pages 134/135 of the coursebook.

to put forward • to make small adjustments • to officially approve • to work out • to create a model or representation of

Verb	Synonym	Collocation
to come together		
to simulate		
to pose		
to clear		
to fine-tune		

8 Edit the text, improving its fluency and making it more readable, by replacing the word *problem* with a synonym (e.g. *dilemma*) or a pronoun (e.g. *it*). Use a thesaurus to find appropriate synonyms. More than one solution is possible.

We were unaware of the problem until week 20, when we were more than halfway through the project. The problem first came to our attention when the client examined a prototype and then claimed that we weren't meeting the specifications according to the contract. The problem was that they had changed their requirements, but only informed one engineer who left our company for another job only two weeks later. We didn't anticipate any problem to arise at that late stage, so we had allowed much of our staff to go on scheduled leave. How did we deal with the problem? We outsourced the problem to specialists. To avoid the problem in the future, I suggest that the specification version is always stated in the contract, and that we always do a final check of the specifications with the client before we begin any engineering. In the end, this problem has cost us both time and money, and has damaged the relationship with a long-standing client.

> **Tip** Native US English speakers only use the word *problem* if a negative situation has actually developed, such as the situations described in tracks 8 and 9 of the coursebook. Before that point, the word *issue* is commonly used.

9 Label the graph, then prepare a short description. It is not necessary to use all the terms in the box. Pay close attention to the verb tenses.

horizontal axis • vertical axis • gradual • sharp • dramatic • steady • rise • jump • drop • decline • stagnate

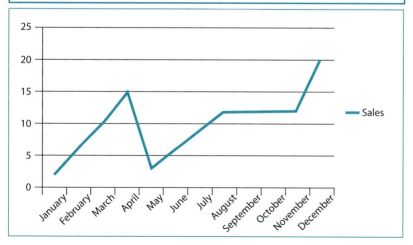

Unit **2** Business processes 15

10 At the water cooler you bump into a colleague who missed a meeting at which a colleague introduced a major initiative. Outline the most important points for your coworker, and try to use forms of the phrases on page 21 in the coursebook ("Reporting orally"). Record your summary.

43 a) Listen to an example answer and see whether you included the same kind of information.

b) Listen again. Can you identify the idioms in the audio that have the same meanings as the phrases?

a very exciting event: ....

the depth of the situation: ....

to have a heavy workload to manage: ....

c) Read the audio transcript on pages 67 and 68 and identify the phrases that Jarrett uses to express interest and keep the conversation going while Werner is providing details about the meeting.

....
....
....

> **Did you know?**
> The water cooler (*Trinkwasserspender*) commonly serves as an informal meeting place for employees in U.S. offices. Topics discussed while employees take a short break to get water can range from popular culture to personal, company, and industry news.

11 Translate the German sentences into English.

1 Obwohl die Käufer zahlreiche Verbesserungsvorschläge machten, aktualisierte die Firma ihr System nicht. Daraufhin sanken die Verkaufszahlen.

....
....

2 Die Behauptung, dass unser bevorzugter Zulieferer Firmeninterna weitergegeben habe, wurde von einem Mitbewerber aufgestellt. Nachdem sich herausgestellt hatte, dass die Behauptung keine Grundlage hatte, zog der Mitbewerber sein Angebot zurück.

....
....

Project management 3

Unit checklist
- discuss schedules and clarify next steps
- request and examine a Proposal for Services
- read about Scrum and knowledge management

1 Match the verbs to the prepositions, then use the correct forms to complete the sentences.

1	pleased	a	to
2	follow up	b	in
3	partner	c	out
4	contribute	d	about
5	hammer	e	on

1 A: What was the feedback from head office?

B: Well, they were very .... the positive response. Now all the two sides need to do is .... the details.

2 A: What happened? I thought we were going to ask Dominic's team to .... the project?

B: We did. Unfortunately, they didn't .... the request in a timely manner, so we were forced to turn to another team that has less experience but much more enthusiasm.

3 A: Could you describe their involvement?

B: They .... the initial study as well as the final report and presentation.

> **Did you know?**
> In the coursebook, Yves wishes Ellen "happy holidays" for good reason: In some English-speaking countries, wishing someone a "Merry Christmas" may be seen as culturally insensitive. It shouldn't be assumed that everyone is a Christian or celebrates Christmas. Use the non-religious greetings "Happy Holidays" or "Season's Greetings" instead.

2 **Listen to the audio, then complete the sentences. In a second step, explain which verb form was used to express the concrete or tentative plans and why.**
🔊 44

1 According to the job description, the trainee ....
   ....

2 In the coming months, Zara ....
   ....

3 Tomorrow, Ellen and her colleagues ....
   ....

4 Next week, Zara ....
   ....

5 On a weekly basis, Zara ....
   ....

6 On Wednesday, Ellen and/or her colleagues ....
   ....

7 When they meet Zara on Wednesday, Bill and Yves ....
   ....

3 **Match the sentence halves, then identify in which situations (a–c) they would fit best.**

1 Before we go	a	step by step?
2 Could you explain this	b	for a moment …
3 I hear	c	any further, let me make sure I've understood.
4 Can you spell	d	what you're saying, but …
5 Just thinking aloud	e	it out for me?
6 If I understand	f	you correctly, …

a to confirm information already stated: sentences ....
b to request clarification on a point: sentences ....
c to respond by giving a suggestion or a contrast: sentences ....

18 Unit **3** Project management

Respond to the information from a colleague using the details in the thought bubbles as well as the matched phrases above. It is possible to use a phrase more than once. You can solve the task in writing or orally, e.g. by recording your answers.

1

Since it was a time-sensitive matter, we decided to ignore the standard internal approval process and proceed.

The mandatory internal approval process ensures that vendor selection is carried out appropriately. He/she has clearly disregarded company policy and this could result in significant consequences for me and my department.

2

Well, the project has three well-defined phases, but each phase is dependent on the successful completion of four sub-tasks.

Further detail is necessary. None of the project documentation details the sub-tasks.

3

We've hit some unexpected roadblocks, so we expect to implement the revised policy in mid-February.

This information comes as a complete surprise – the deadline is January 12!

4

We've found that the scope of the project exceeds the current capacity of our team.

This doesn't make sense. The team hired a new full-time employee only two months ago.

Unit **3** Project management 19

4 Translate the sentences into English.

1. Das folgende Leistungsangebot basiert auf den Informationen, die im Rahmen des Telefonats am 13. November 20xx von Frau Ellen Wagner von Schulze Automotive Holding GmbH & Co. KG zur Verfügung gestellt wurden, sowie der Ausschreibung vom 14. November 20xx.

   ....
   ....
   ....

2. Der Auftraggeber hat dem Auftragnehmer sämtliche für die Untersuchung erforderlichen Unterlagen unverzüglich zur Verfügung zu stellen.

   ....
   ....

3. Bis zu 20 % der Gesamtrechnung (inkl. MwSt.) werden für Nebenkosten in Rechnung gestellt, die im Rahmen von projektbezogenen Reisen anfallen.

   ....
   ....

4. Der endgültige Projektbericht bzw. die Projektergebnisse einschließlich sämtlicher Reproduktionen und Übersetzungen in andere Sprachen dürfen Dritten nur mit ausdrücklicher schriftlicher Genehmigung von Energy Consulting Ltd offengelegt werden.

   ....
   ....
   ....

> **Tip** The term *incidental expenses* is often used in contracts and reimbursement policies to refer to out-of-pocket expenses that arise during travel.

5 Cross out any expressions that don't fit the sentences.

1. Would you be willing to give me a ballpark figure / give me your bottom line / be on the same page?
2. We keep our expenses / ballpark figure / bottom line low by flying economy class and staying in hotels that partner with our company.
3. I don't feel the pinch / we're on the same page / we're successfully meeting our benchmarks.
4. We'd like to bring a participant / a facilitator / a benchmark on board to support the project.

6 Complete the phone conversation. Most gaps have multiple possible answers.

A: Thank you for . . . . How . . . . help you?

B: Am I . . . . Nicole O'Reilly?

A: Yes, this is . . . .

B: Hello, Ms O'Reilly, this is Thomas Olbermann from Olbermann International. I'm calling . . . . a potential project. I got your name from Olivia Gomez. I . . . . that your team . . . . some research for her company last year. Are you the . . . . person to speak to about an upcoming project?

A: Yes, I'm the team . . . .

B: Great. Well, we're a small German talent recruitment agency and we're . . . . the possibility of expansion into the Eastern European market. We'd like for you to research the recruitment market . . . . our niche – engineers within the energy industry.

A: That's . . . . something we can help you with. What we would need from you is . . . .

B: We're . . . . today, so it should reach you shortly. Our company policy . . . . that we . . . . three separate bids before . . . . a decision. In the meantime, would you be . . . . to send us some information about the key research services . . . . as well as some client references? Olivia told me about the work you . . . . for her company – they were very . . . ., so we already know of one . . . . customer.

A: Yes, of course, I'd be happy to.

B: One more question: assuming we . . . . to work with you, when . . . . begin? What we don't want is for a competitor to enter the market even weeks ahead of us.

A: . . . ., I can't answer that until I see the RFP and gain a better understanding of the project's . . . .

B: Of course. I . . . . You can expect the RFP later today via email. Thanks very much for your time.

7 Based on the information in exercise 6, draft a short RFP. Add details as needed. Use the RFP on page 35 of the coursebook as a model.

....
....
....
....
....
....
....

8 Your company is implementing Scrum methods. You have a new intern who will be working for the company during the transition. In two or three sentences, summarize the article on Scrum on page 37 of the coursebook in order to familiarize your intern with the concept.

....
....
....
....
....

9 Find words in the article on page 37 of the coursebook that mean the following:

1 (v.) to grow, to develop: ....
2 (v.) to prepare the first version of something, usually a document: ....
3 (adj.) limited, restricted: ....
4 (adj.) focused or grouped at a specific point rather than distributed over space or time: ....
5 (v.) to force someone to face and deal with something or someone: ....
6 (adj.) unchanging: ....
7 (v.) to collect something from various sources: ....
8 (adj.) completely or fully necessary: ....

Now choose four of the words and use any form of the words in a sentence that is relevant for your work. As an extra challenge, use the verb forms for concrete and tentative plans covered on page 33 of the coursebook.

over to you

....
....
....
....
....
....

10 The unit provides examples of three different ways that hyphens (-) are used in English. First, identify which phrases use hyphens …

a	… as a way of forming a compound modifier (adjective).	1	kick-off meeting
b	… as a way of forming a noun.	2	non-critical tasks
c	… as a way of attaching a common prefix to an adjective.	3	time-consuming project
		4	business-like courtesy
		5	role-plays
		6	daily stand-up meetings
		7	cross-functional teams

Now explain the difference between the two pairs of sentences.

> The project was very time intensive.
> It was a very time-intensive project.

> The consultant we hired is well known as an expert in Scrum methods.
> The well-known consultant we hired for the project is an expert in Scrum methods.

....
....
....
....

Unit **3** Project management

4 International teams

Unit checklist
- communicate about operations and logistics
- practise teleconferencing language
- practise dealing with conflict
- examine cultural differences

1 Many adjectives used to talk about logistics can also be used in other aspects of business. Cross out the noun that does not form a common collocation.

1	collaborative	team / effort / mentality / suggestion
2	interim	director / idea / office space / goal
3	real-time	process / issue / monitoring / updates
4	leading	provider / producer / process / company
5	state-of-the-art	decision / technology / devices / software

2 You are new to a long-standing international team that primarily communicates via email and teleconference. You are participating in your first teleconference. Write out notes for a brief introduction you could use to introduce yourself to the team during an introduction round, then practise it aloud. If applicable, use some collocations from exercise 1.

over to you

3 In a conference call with two or three additional speakers, you are acting as the facilitator and must respond to several situations that arise. Read the speech bubble, then listen and respond spontaneously. Several answers are possible.

1

1 Status: inland storage containers

> First on our agenda is the interim storage containers. Raymond, could you give us an update?

Listen to track 45, then respond:

....

....

2

2 Iota Inc. – inland water shipment

> Let's see, right. Next we wanted to talk about the coordination of our inland water shipment for Iota Inc.

Listen to track 46, then respond:

....

....

3

3 Sanders project

> Okay, I've described what we need in detail. Who can take on the Sanders project?

Listen to track 47, then respond:

....

....

Tip The official English translations of the names of federal agencies can usually be found directly on the website of each respective agency. For an example, see http://www.bsh.de.

Unit **4** International teams

4 Anke Kern uses several informal phrases during the teleconference (listen to tracks 14 and 15 or see transcripts 14 and 15 on pages 138 and 139 of the coursebook). Match the sentence halves to form more formal phrases, then decide in which situation they could best be applied.

1	I apologize for the delay;	a		so let's try to get through the agenda as quickly as possible.
2	I know we all have a lot on our plates,	b		and we can continue now.
3	I apologize, but could we all stay on the line	c		what precisely do you mean?
4	I think we're able	d		and take a two-minute break so that I can retrieve the documentation from my office?
5	Mr Henry, would you mind explaining	e		as brief as possible.
6	I'd like to keep this	f		speak with my assistant.
7	Please excuse me a moment while I	g		what you mean by 'expertise'?
8	When you say 'expertise,'	h		staying on the line. Now we can move on.
9	It seems as if the technical problem has been resolved	i		to continue now.
10	All right, thanks for	j		thanks for your patience.

1 Upon beginning the telecon: "OK, let's keep this short."

   ....

2 Upon moving forward after an interruption due to a connection problem: "So, let's go on."

   ....

3 Upon hearing a term that might be unclear: "Just to clarify, what exactly do you mean by 'expertise'?"

   ....

4 Upon needing to pause to get something or converse with someone: "Could you just hang on a second, please?"

   ....

5 Upon continuing the conversation: "Sorry!"

   ....

5 Underline the sentence beginnings that are often used to politely request that others change their behaviour.

> You need to … · It would be helpful if … · Next time, could you … · I would appreciate it if … · I noticed that … · Is it necessary for you to …? · It doesn't seem that … · You should … · You can't … · I think that it's better if you … · Could you …? · Why do you …?

What words do the polite phrases have in common? ....

....

What words do the direct and less polite phrases have in common? ....

....

6 Rewrite the statements using the polite phrases you identified in exercise 5. Several answers are possible.

1 You must be more careful when talking to clients. You don't have enough experience yet.

....

....

2 It was a bad decision to take that action without my approval.

....

3 The document wasn't attached to your email.

....

....

4 It is not acceptable that the Wi-Fi was down and no one notified me.

....

5 Next time, don't send a confirmation without approval from production.

....

....

6 You didn't clearly communicate the action we were supposed to take, so don't blame us if the task wasn't carried out by the deadline.

....

....

7 Substitute the underlined words in each sentence with synonymous words or phrases.

1   A: I find it extremely <u>annoying</u> when he doesn't communicate what he needs. After all, I'm here to support him!

    ....

    B: I <u>suppose</u> it's difficult to wrap up a project if there's a lack of communication.

    ....

2   A: We've got to <u>settle</u> that matter today.

    ....

    B: That's for sure. I heard from head office that management is getting a little <u>fed up</u> with the quantity of goods that is being spoiled due to our logistical errors with the temperature-controlled containers.

    ....

3   A: Everyone seems to be <u>drawing conclusions</u> regarding the implementation of the Wi-Fi-based RFID system.

    ....

    B: I hear you. Since we're such a small company it will revolutionize the way we do business. I would definitely <u>appreciate</u> more details.

    ....

8 Translate the statements into English. Use the new vocabulary and idioms from Part B of the coursebook.

1   Es ist unnötig, ihn in Verlegenheit zu bringen.

    ....

2   Am besten besprecht ihr beiden das in Ruhe.

    ....

3   Ich schätze, ich habe dich/Sie falsch verstanden.

    ....

4   Offenbar hatten wir einen schlechten Start miteinander.

    ....

9 Read the statements below. For each set of statements, find an alternative that you feel comfortable using, yet which bridges the two styles. Multiple answers are possible.

Clear		Tactful
Let's talk about the sales report.		We really need to run through these figures. Is now a good time?
Call Francine and see if she can meet on Tuesday.		Maybe we should call Francine and see if she can meet on Tuesday?
That was a terrible decision.		Unfortunately, that decision was not in the best interest of the company.
I have no time today. I am very busy right now.		Would you mind coming back later? I'm just in the middle of something.

10 Test your understanding of the article on page 47 of the coursebook. Read the statements and decide if they are true (t) or false (f). Correct any false statements.

1 Gill Woodman is a sociologist at the Ludwig Maximilian University Munich.
   ☐ ....

2 "Would you mind …" is the beginning of a request in which the speaker expects a request to be carried out.
   ☐ ....

3 When making requests, Germans can sound unfriendly and aggressive to native English speakers because the amount of detail they include.
   ☐ ....

4 Spontaneous responses are more often given by the British.
   ☐ ....

5 Because they often use prepared phrases to make requests, the British tend to sound insincere to Germans.
   ☐ ....

> **Did you know?**
>
> *Excuse me* is a term frequently used by native English speakers. It often doesn't take on the meaning of *Ich bitte um Verzeihung/es tut mir leid*, but rather simply *Entschuldigung!* similar to *pardon* or *sorry*. In addition to being used in business, it is also often used when someone bumps into another person or walks in front of them and blocks their way or view, such as in a store.

5 Sustainable business

Unit checklist
- explore sustainability
- review financial performance
- pitch financial services
- practise business storytelling and reporting

1 Use the timeline to describe developments at TrinkO. Use the simple past, past continuous, and past perfect to relate past events.

Timeline events:
- 2005: developing a new sports drink / product breakthrough
- 2008: searching for partnering distributors in Western Europe
- 2000: company founded
- 2002: commenced sales in Poland
- 2001–2003: successful sales in Germany, Austria, Switzerland
- 2006: commenced sales in the Czech Republic
- 2009: established key contacts in Asia, started selling in Japan and Vietnam
- 2011: approached by a potential partner in South America, redirected efforts to SA

TrinkO was selling products successfully in German-speaking countries when it …

30 Unit **5** Sustainable business

2 Decide which nouns could be used to form collocations. The nouns can be used more than once.

> production • output • net income • earnings • earnings per share • prices • investment • operating result • sales

1 The company reported **an increase in** ....
....

2 Unfortunately, ...
.... **was/were down** from the previous year.

3 Last year, (the) ....
.... **amounted to** 8 billion euros.

3 Use the information from the table below and the words and phrases to form sentences.

> over the previous year • by just under/over xx euros • by just under/over xx % • roughly

	Last year	This year
Sales	24.7 billion euros	28.1 billion euros
Earnings	12.6 billion euros	13.5 billion euros
Share price	2.30 euros	2.12 euros

Tip When discussing figures, short words, particularly adverbs and prepositions such as *by*, *to*, *up*, *down*, *of*, and *from*, are key to identifying the movement or change. See transcript 23 on page 141 of the coursebook for several examples.

....
....
....
....
....
....
....
....
....
....

4 Complete each dialogue. Use either the third conditional or a mixed conditional statement or question.

1. A: Where would you be now if you had accepted that job in Scotland five years ago?

   B: ....

2. A: If you had noticed the "creative accounting" before the audit, what would you have done?

   B: ....
   All in all, it might have saved us from insolvency.

3. A: ....

   B: No, if we hadn't applied for and received the government subsidy, we wouldn't have been able to invest in new assets such as buildings and equipment. No other option was available.

4. A: ....

   B: The composition of our workforce would look very different today if we hadn't been committed to promoting social equity – we would have less young talent and fewer minority employees.

5. A: Would our profits be significantly higher if we had licensed out production to a company in Pakistan?

   B: ....

6. A: If the company hadn't gone public in 2012, would we have been able to raise enough capital?

   B: ....

5 Use track 24 or the transcript on pages 141–142 of the coursebook to complete the puzzle.

1: to make a company smaller (paragraph 4)
2: to wind up a business, usually converting assets to pay creditors (paragraph 5)
3: significant positions of power (2 words; paragraph 2)
4: there was a significant drop in sales among the key customer base (4 words; paragraph 4)
5: someone who is the first to do or develop something (paragraph 1)
6: to negatively affect and weaken (paragraph 4)
7: to be the first to develop or use something (paragraph 2)

Did you know?

A common phrase in English is *Hindsight is always 20/20*.
Perfect vision is often referred to as 20/20, which is pronounced *twenty–twenty*.

6 Which background information should a prospective buyer or client communicate to a potential seller (service provider or manufacturer) when he or she requires a specific product or service? Make a checklist.

....
....
....

7 Now listen to a prospective buyer describing his company's needs. Does the description include all the points you listed above? Does the buyer include additional information that you did not include on your list?

🎧 48

....
....
....

Listen again. Identify standard phrases that might be helpful for a buyer to use when briefing a potential seller.

....
....
....
....
....

Unit **5** Sustainable business 33

8 Look at the flow charts on page 57 of the coursebook. If you were the seller, how would you adapt them if you
   a) had an opportunity to do a spontaneous "elevator pitch" in one minute to a prospective client you had never previously met;
   b) had received all the concrete specifications in advance; or
   c) had to pitch a repeat client?

Map out possible scenarios in the form of diagrams, then practise the ones that you think would be the most realistic for you and your business.

over to you

9 Service providers and manufacturers often give references, also referred to as "actual examples" and "case studies" in the coursebook, to prospective clients or customers in order to illustrate their capabilities and completed projects and/or to name satisfied customers.

Use the notes below to draft a reference based on the services requested in exercise 7. Listen to the audio again or refer to the transcript on page 69.

the client operates • to conduct/carry out a study • to explore the feasibility • to assess and update the findings • to take something into account • the findings show/illustrate/reveal • to recover investment costs

Findings:
- *if a partial replacement, costs are recovered within 10 years*
- *if a full replacement, costs are recovered within 22 years*

Did you know?

References often use the passive voice to describe work completed.

34 Unit **5** Sustainable business

10 You work for a small biopharmaceutical company and are responsible for keeping an eye on developments in the industry. In a meeting with your colleagues, you must present a short verbal summary of what was communicated by the CEO in the introduction to MorphoSys's annual report. Use track 26 or the transcript on page 143 of the coursebook. Write down some notes you could use to give a short summary, then practise what you would say.

> the company reported that • according to the company, …

....
....
....
....
....

11 Translate the sentences into English.

1 Wenn wir mehr Kapital hätten aufbringen können, hätten wir unsere Aktivitäten in Übersee ausweiten können.

   ....

2 Wir hätten mehr unternehmen müssen, um unsere Zukunftsfähigkeit zu verbessern.

   ....

3 Entschuldigen Sie, da habe ich mich nicht klar ausgedrückt.

   ....

4 Wir sind ganz zufrieden mit dem, was wir bisher gesehen haben.

   ....

5 Ich verstehe Ihre Besorgnis.

   ....

6 Gut, dass Sie das ansprechen.

   ....

6 Managing people

Unit checklist
- debate the pros and cons of workplace conditions
- recount an HR incident
- practise giving feedback
- discuss assessment methods

1 Complete the employees' statements about their workplace and perks with the phrases below. More than one answer may be possible.

> on the one hand • the downside is • on the whole • has made a big difference • there are a lot of positive things to say • on the other hand • to me, the biggest perk • overall

1. "............................. about the workplace conditions and our corporate culture. .... the long working hours we need to put in."

2. "............................., when working from home I've always been accessible by phone. ...., I agree that face-to-face interaction can't be replaced."

3. "............................. is the building loan subsidy. We expect to buy our own home within the next two years."

4. "............................., if the company wants to remain competitive, it must improve its compensation package in order to attract top talent in the field."

5. "............................., the possibility of participating in the retirement fund savings plan .... regarding my decision to continue working with the company. With the help of that plan and some very lucky private investments, I'll be able to retire when I'm 65 – I'm already counting the days!"

2 Group the expressions you can use to argue your opinion according to their purposes. Then think of a situation in your workplace at the moment for which you need to give your opinion. Use some of the words or phrases to make your argument.

> my understanding is • said differently • as I see it • taking every aspect into account • I've been told • in other words • I am aware • from my perspective • if we take a step back, we can see that • all things considered • personally • to put it another way

To give your own view	....
To restate an idea	....
To look at the big picture	....
To state the information you know about a situation	....

3 Use reported speech to restate what you were told. Add *I* or *me* as needed.

1 "Did you ask Doris about next year's training opportunities?"

   She wanted to know ....

2 "Why don't you talk with Carla about it?"

   Yesterday he suggested ....

3 "We'll announce the pay cuts soon."

   Last week she told me ....

4 "Since the twins were born, I've been having difficulty managing my work-life balance."

   She said that since the twins ....
   ....

5 "No, sorry, I'm not able to volunteer on Saturdays due to family commitments. I'm only available to volunteer in the evenings."

He said ....

....

6 "I'm going to change jobs in December."

Early this year she told me ....

4 Whether or not changes are necessary in reported speech depends on when the statement was made and when the person reports what they heard.
You spoke with a colleague on Tuesday. Now it's Thursday. Rewrite the statements using reported speech and shifting the tenses and adverbs as needed.

1 "Tomorrow I have my performance evaluation."

Gillian said ....

2 "Yesterday I successfully closed a deal with a new client."

On Tuesday Gillian told me ....

3 "Last week we had a meeting with the team leader who will be filling in for Carla while she's on maternity leave."

Gillian said ....

....

You spoke with a colleague in December. Now it's February. Rewrite the statements using reported speech and shifting the tenses and adverbs as needed.

4 "Last year our company adopted a generous long-service bonus policy."

Frank said ....

5 "In two months I'm attending a trade fair in Barcelona."

In December Frank told me ....

6 "In February I'm going to take two weeks' holiday."

Frank mentioned ....

Did you know?

In English-speaking workplaces, it's typical for supervisors to give positive feedback if they think a job is going well, not only negative feedback about unsatisfactory performance. If English-speaking colleagues don't get any feedback, they may wonder what is wrong with their performance.

5 First, decide by whom the statement in the first column would be made during an assessment, an appraiser (A) or an employee (E).
Then match the statement to the related feedback, question or response.

1	"Thank you for mentioning that point. It was a rewarding challenge and I am happy that I was able to hit the ground running." ☐	a	"I'm glad you brought that up. I agree, actually, and I learned a good lesson from the situation. I guess I was too embarrassed to admit I was unsure. In the subsequent project, I did ask for lots of guidance, and everyone was just great."
2	"For example, when you continued working but were unsure how to proceed, you could have consulted with your colleagues or supervisor." ☐	b	"I've been particularly impressed by your ability to complete the research started by the person who was in the job before you. It can be very difficult to start mid-way through."
3	"So what you're saying is that there is one main issue that we need to deal with: improving communication among you and your fellow team members." ☐	c	"How do you see your performance over the past year?"
4	"Well, my perspective might be a little bit one-sided, of course, but I'm actually quite pleased with how things have been going." ☐	d	"I did my best to complete my tasks, but I wasn't able to judge if the team was pleased with my work or if something was wrong. Particularly as a new hire, it was difficult to tell if my performance was satisfactory or disappointing."

> **Tip** *Performance review, annual assessment, yearly evaluation, annual appraisal,* and *performance appraisal,* along with other variations, can all be used to refer to the yearly meeting between supervisors and employees, or HR representatives and employees.

6 If you were discussing your performance with a supervisor, which phrases could you use to acknowledge positive and negative feedback before giving your response? Brainstorm some examples.

I appreciate that feedback very much ...

1 "Your work has been outstanding!"
2 "We need to see substantial improvement in that area over the next year."
3 "We noticed you had some difficulty meeting the deadline."
4 "It's clear that the team enjoys working under your leadership."

Unit **6** Managing people 39

7 Each CD track contains a piece of feedback and an example reaction. Imagine you are at your annual appraisal. Listen to the first piece of feedback. Pause the CD to give your spontaneous reaction. Then listen to the example response. After repeating the process for each track, listen to the recordings again and identify key words or phrases you could use at your next appraisal.

- Performance review areas
- Interpersonal skills
- Initiating action
- Technical skills

8 You're sharing with a colleague or your partner what the appraiser said during the performance review. Refer to transcrips 49–54 on page 70 and write an email. Revise reported speech by restating the feedback you received.

9 You are a supervisor conducting the appraisal of a new hire. For each statement the new hire makes, think of an appropriate open-ended question you could ask in response.

1 "Although I've tried to cultivate strong relationships with members of the team, I don't feel as if I've made much progress."

....

2 "Surprisingly, I've had difficulty managing my workload. I'm often in the office till 8 or 9 pm."

....

3 "Quite frequently, the tasks I'm assigned don't correspond to my education or experience. They are time-consuming, but far beneath my capabilities."

....

4 "On a positive note, the in-house training has been absolutely outstanding and I hope to be able to participate in future programmes that are offered."

....

10 Use your own words to provide a synonym or definition for the collocations used in Part C of the coursebook.

1 to employ an assessment method (p. 68, exercise 1 questions)
   to use a specific process to measure or evaluate something

2 to reconcile two interests (p. 68, interview subheading)

....

3 to be entangled in internal relationships (p. 68, interview)

....

4 to benchmark a candidate against a standard (p. 68, interview)

....

5 to assess the degree to which (p. 68, interview)

....

6 infectious enthusiasm (p. 69, exercise 3)

....

7 the degree of convergence (p. 69, exercise 4)

....

11 Your company is considering "Job-Man Fitting" audits. Employees have been invited to learn about the process and express their opinions. Reread the article on page 68 of the coursebook and the related information on page 69. Make some notes and formulate your thoughts about this kind of audit. Use expressions from exercise 2 on page 37 of this workbook.

over to you

....
....
....
....
....
....
....
....

12 Translate the sentences into English.

1. Trotz meiner Versuche, die Kommunikation aufrechtzuerhalten, hatte ich zunehmend das Gefühl, dass Informationen an mir vorbeigeschleust wurden.

   ....
   ....

2. Das wird viel länger dauern, als Sie erwarten. Der Vorgang bringt eine Menge Papierkrieg mit sich.

   ....

3. Ich habe gehört, ein Teammitglied habe gesagt, ich würde nicht richtig mitziehen.

   ....

4. Offensichtlich gab es Schwierigkeiten mit der Kommunikation, während er von Zuhause aus gearbeitet hat.

   ....

5. Wir müssen evaluieren, in welchem Maß jährliche Mitarbeitergespräche die Leistung verbessern.

   ....

Meeting demand 7

Unit checklist
- contrast marketing practices
- practise networking
- discuss intellectual property issues
- handle formal correspondence
- discuss brands and social marketing

1 Which of the 4 Ps is addressed with each question?

a ☐ place
b ☐ price
c ☐ product
d ☐ promotion

1 Which discounts, if any, should we offer?
2 What do our customers expect and need?
3 Are TV advertisements more effective than social media?
4 Where do our customers expect to find the product or service in the market?
5 What features and benefits do we offer?
6 Are our customers' budgets sensitive?
7 What is the best media outlet to reach our target market?
8 Which distribution channel is most effective?

2 First determine whether each statement is a recurring behaviour (B) or a state (S). Then rewrite the sentences about the past using *used to* and/or *would*.

> **Tip** *Would* can be used synonymously with *used to* in statements (not questions) only when referring to a recurring activity or behaviour and not a past state. If referring to a state, *used to* or the simple past are required.
> Activity or behaviour: We *would* distribute flyers at all the shops. / We *used to* distribute flyers at all the shops. / In the past we *distributed* flyers at all the shops.
> State: We *used to* have 12 stores. / In the past we *had* 12 stores.

1 ☐ In the past we only offered discounts to our key clients.
....
2 ☐ Years ago, compliance was extremely vague and never monitored.
....
3 ☐ In those days we didn't hire service dealers.
....
4 ☐ Before we extended our warranty, some customers called every week to complain.
....
5 ☐ We had a complicated price structure for over 10 years.
....

3 Writers can sometimes get lost in their sentence clauses. First make the sentences more succinct. Then note what you changed and how.

1 The testing which is carried out on site is the optimal way to test new equipment.

   ....

2 Certification that is necessary for compliance requires a process which is long.

   ....

3 Companies which focus on promoting sustainability have better results in the market.

   ....

4 Contacts that were made at the speed networking event resulted in clients who were new.

   ....

Now look at a letter or email you recently wrote. Can you make some of the sentences more succinct by revising them in a similar way?

4 You're part of the sales team for the TRX 5000. Take comprehensive notes while listening. Then listen again and add any points you missed or correct any mistakes. What percentage of the information were you able to record correctly the first time you heard it?

....
....
....
....
....
....
....
....
....
....

5 **Read your notes or listen once more to answer the following questions:**

1 Which topics does the speaker address and in what order?

   ....

2 Which of the four Ps are addressed and how?

   ....

   ....

   ....

   ....

3 In what ways does the speaker acknowledge that the topic might be controversial?

   ....

   ....

   ....

4 List the idioms with the following meanings:

   something to think about: ....

   better value for the money: ....

   to learn about something informally: ....

6 **Use the correct form of the words to complete the story. Not all words will be used.**

> cease • claim • contest • file • infringe • lose • scare • settle • win • withdraw

A competitor .... trademark infringement and demanded that we .... production of our top-selling product. We .... the claim, of course. In the end, we .... the right to use our design. It turns out that we could have simply ignored their .... and desist letter. Even before the competitor had sent the letter, they had .... the trademark application they had .... for the design in question. They were merely using a .... tactic – or they received very poor legal advice.

Unit **7** Meeting demand   45

7 **By drawing lines, join the clauses to form sentences.**

Not only did they	filed the trademark application	been awarded.
No sooner had they	do SMEs stand their ground	they also gave it a similar name.
Under no circumstances	unveil a nearly identical product,	infringe the copyright.
Never before have	does our use of the image	acknowledge responsibility.
Only rarely	such high monetary damages	against industry giants.
In no way	should you	than we received a letter from their lawyer.

8 **Lines 5–12 of the article on page 81 of the coursebook illustrate a professional and polite register that isn't too formal. Using lines 5–12 as an example, rewrite the other posts quoted in the article.**

....
....
....
....
....
....
....
....
....
....
....

Did you know?
When used in regard to language, the term *register* includes the formality of the language, the structures used to form phrases and sentences, and the choice of vocabulary.

9 Decide for which scenario(s) a formal letter from a lawyer may not be the best course of action when trying to protect a brand and control an image.

1. an extremely harsh online review has criticized your product or service
2. false claims about your product are being made in the advertisements of a competitor
3. a trademarked name and/or a copyrighted image is being used by a private person in a blog without your company's permission
4. a competitor in the same field is using a slogan or logo similar to yours
5. a shop claims it uses your product to make something it sells

For one of the scenarios you selected above, write the letter you might send first before taking legal action. Use a register similar to the one you used in exercise 8.

over to you

10 Translate the sentences into English.

1. Es nicht so genau zu nehmen birgt ein höheres Risiko.

   ....

2. Ralf ist ein gewissenhafter Angestellter, der entscheidend dazu beigetragen hat, den Datenschutz für die Nutzer unserer mobilen App zu gewährleisten.

   ....
   ....

3. Wir hatten die Unterlassungsanordnung kaum verschickt, da kamen schon die ersten Anrufe von den Medien.

   ....
   ....

4. Sie sollten auf keinen Fall antworten, ohne vorher juristischen Rat von unserem Firmenanwalt eingeholt zu haben.

   ....
   ....

5. Wir bestätigen hiermit den Eingang Ihres Schreibens vom 19. April.

   ....

6. Unvorhergesehene Umstände haben es uns unmöglich gemacht, innerhalb des vorgegebenen Zeitrahmens zu antworten.

   ....

8 Public relations

Unit checklist
- discuss codes of business conduct
- handle difficult questions
- explore corporate social responsibility
- write a press release
- deal with social media for PR

1 A new colleague has come on board just as you are preparing for an internal audit in your company. To bring her up to speed, prepare a short outline of what the audit involves and the steps your team needs to take to prepare.

over to you

Aim of the internal audit:

....
....
....
....
....
....

Steps required to prepare for the internal audit:

....
....
....
....
....
....

2 Bernd Jung, compliance officer at A&G Fashion, speaks to the press. He organizes his thoughts in a structure commonly used for press statements. Listen to track 37 or read his statement on pages 147–148 of the coursebook and identify how he structures his statement.

1 The company's reaction – shock and sadness. ....
2 ....
3 ....
4 ....
5 ....

3 Think of a crisis situation that would require your company to make a statement to the press. Then write your own statement. Use key phrases from the transcript on pages 147–148 of the coursebook.

over to you

Let me say that ....

The findings ....

I'd like to make it clear that ....

We pledge to ....

In the next few days ....

> **Did you know?**
> The term *damage control* is often used when dealing with a crisis affecting public relations. It refers to keeping the harm to the company as minimal as possible.

4 Write a definition or synonym for each verb from the unit.

to condemn: ....

to condone: ....

to disclose: ....

to exert: ....

to field: ....

to flag: ....

to pledge: ....

Complete the sentences. Use the verbs listed above.

1 While he was .... questions, the company spokesperson .... that the company would take steps to investigate the disaster to the fullest extent possible.

2 We do not .... that kind of unethical behaviour – on the contrary, we .... it.

3 After an employee died while working in the factory, the deputy mayor .... her influence so that the company would .... the results of past internal audits. The findings revealed that unsafe working conditions had been .... years before.

Unit **8** Public relations 49

5 Group the verbs according to whether they require the infinitive or gerund to follow them, or whether they can be followed by either.

> suggest • seem • remember • intend • claim • forget • imagine • promise • discuss • appreciate • stop • consider • regret • fail • try

infinitive	gerund	either infinitive or gerund

Those that can be followed by either undergo a change in meaning. Write sentences to illustrate and explain the change in meaning.

Verb: ....

1 Infinitive: ....

 Meaning: ....

2 Gerund: ....

 Meaning: ....

Verb: ....

1 Infinitive: ....

 Meaning: ....

2 Gerund: ....

 Meaning: ....

6 It is often necessary to define words or categories for business partners. Listen to the audio and identify the phrase that the speaker uses to signal his definition.

....

50 Unit **8** Public relations

List additional signal phrases you could use.

....

....

Now think of several terms or categories that you often use in your job and formulate definitions for clients or other external business partners.

7 Unscramble the sentences to form responses which evaluate cautiously.

1 customer satisfaction / I would / linked to / say that turnover / is most closely

....

2 a larger / it helps to / some extent / reporting and PR strategy / if it is part of

....

3 supply chain / on the / to make the / more visible / whole, we need

....

4 appear as if / large, it will / by and / the manufacturer / to hide / has something

....

5 practical purposes, / they do / some degree / tend to / for all / help to

....

Now match the sentences to the following questions.

a	Is developing KPI reporting metrics the best option for solving client-related concerns?
b	If a manufacturer does not make its supply chain transparent, does it risk losing customer trust?
c	Do all CSR programmes have a positive impact on the populations they intend to serve, or is it merely a corporate PR scheme?
d	Which KPI has been the most indicative of customer satisfaction?
e	What would you say we should do to address customers' concerns?

8 Use the information to write the first paragraph of a press release (a stand-alone summary containing the key message).

Who: Jupiter Chocolates Ltd.
What: first milestones achieved in three-year project; two of five schools built, staffed; lessons for children take place on a daily basis; adult farming education programmes began last week
Where: Cote d'Ivoire, settlement of 10,000 people; in the south-west
When: May 7, 20xx, 18 months after the project commenced
Why: to support sustainable farming practices through education of farmers; to improve education for children
How: FarmSchool Programme

Then list what additional information you would include in subsequent paragraphs.

....
....
....
....
....

> **Tip** Use the first sentence of a press release or news article to state the most important fact or accomplishment.

9 Study the tweets in exercise 3 on page 91 of the coursebook. Then tick the characteristic(s) that describe them best.

1 The tone can best be described as
- [ ] formal.
- [ ] relaxed.
- [ ] professional.

2 The tweets use
- [ ] complete sentences using correct grammar.
- [ ] phrases.

3 The tweets include
- [ ] mostly abbreviations.
- [ ] mostly full words.

4 Describe the content/message of the tweets in one or two sentences.

....

....

10 Research two or three of your company's competitors. Evaluate their use of social media in regard to frequency, message, register and followers. Your research should include various social media platforms. Write a brief report to your company's CEO which summarizes your findings and makes a recommendation about your company's use of social media.

....

....

....

....

....

....

11 Translate the sentences into English.

1 Wir sind zutiefst erschüttert über die unsicheren Arbeitsbedingungen und den daraus resultierenden Tod von zwei Arbeitern.

....

2 Wir werden alles in unserer Macht Stehende tun, um die Situation sofort zu verbessern.

....

3 Der Ansatz erscheint praktikabel. Dennoch befürchten wir, dass nicht das erhoffte Ergebnis dabei herauskommt.

....

4 Nun ja, das ist eine mittelmäßige Lösung.

....

5 Wussten Sie, dass Ihre Firma Tausende im Jahr sparen kann, wenn sie ihren ökologischen Fußabdruck verkleinert? Nehmen Sie teil an unserem Live-Chat mit Experten, Donnerstag um 9 Uhr. #footprint

....

....

Unit 1–4 Progress check 1

Check your knowledge from Units 1–4. Look at these questions (1–20) and tick the correct answer to each question. You get one point for each correct answer.

Describing your work & dealing with colleagues   Points

1. We are responsible for … with key stakeholders.
   a attending **b** facilitating **c** liaising **d** presenting
2. Are you … from China?
   a firstly **b** initially **c** original **d** originally
3. He prides … in his knowledge of intricate processes.
   a him **b** himself **c** his self **d** his work
4. Our team has worked together … three years.
   a at **b** for **c** since **d** with
5. I'm sure you two just got off on the … foot.
   Why not meet for lunch and talk things over?
   a bad **b** left **c** right **d** wrong

Projects & processes   Points

6. The model was … to the designer's specifications.
   a build **b** built **c** did **d** done
7. Since we're … schedule, the office atmosphere is extremely relaxed.
   a according to **b** ahead of **c** in front of **d** lying within
8. The order is cancelled by the system if the payment … valid.
   a is **b** were **c** wasn't **d** isn't
9. It was such a time-… project; our entire team was relieved when it was over.
   a consuming **b** taking **c** saving **d** costing
10. Due to skyrocketing energy prices, we've really been feeling the ….
    a expenses **b** hammer **c** pinch **d** punch
11. We haven't finalized the agenda ….
    a already **b** now **c** yesterday **d** yet

54 Progress check 1

Discussing possibilities   Points

12 …, bearing those parameters in mind we'd be looking at about 2 euros per unit.
    a Speaking in general **b** Generally speaking
    c Talking in general   **d** Generally talking
13 Assuming we planned to order 500 units, … you give us a quantity discount?
    a can **b** could **c** shall **d** should
14 If we began the simulation earlier, we … enough time to make the necessary adjustments.
    a will have **b** will be having **c** would have
    d would have had
15 Should we recommend … the final phase of the project?
    a to complete **b** handling **c** outsourcing **d** to oversee

Internal communication   Points

16 I hear what you …, but wouldn't it be appropriate to involve the Rotterdam office?
    a 're saying **b** say **c** were saying **d** will say
17 I'd … it if you could copy me in on your messages to the Kiev office.
    a appreciate **b** be connected to you **c** pleasure
    d treasure
18 We've got a lot to discuss in a short amount of time, so let's try not to get ….
    a over-track **b** on-track **c** out-track **d** off-track
19 Sorry, Ms Ivanova, just to …, what exactly do you mean by "automated"?
    a know **b** convince **c** clarify **d** question
20 Let's see what kind of strategy we can come … with to win back one of our key clients.
    a across **b** at **c** up **d** over

Total points: / 20

Unit 5-8 Progress check 2

Check your knowledge of Units 5–8. Look at these questions (1–20) and tick the correct answer to each question. You get one point for each correct answer.

Business decisions & results   Points

1 Before we award them the contract, we need some … of their experience in this particular area.
   a assurance **b** insurance **c** safety **d** security
2 Due to the difficulty we had entering the market, our initial sales results were not ….
   a satisfactory **b** satisfiable **c** satisfied **d** satisfying
3 We … only a few points of sale. That changed after we entered the B2C market.
   a had had **b** have had **c** used to have **d** would have
4 The stable growth of the market segment is in our favour. We should be able to … the investment costs within five years.
   a get back **b** recoup **c** reimburse **d** take back
5 We can't assume that government … will be offered next year, so why not submit an application this year?
   a allowance **b** credits **c** subsidiaries **d** subsidies
6 If we default … our payments, our suppliers may refuse to fill our standing orders.
   a in **b** on **c** to **d** with

Managing personnel   Points

7 We should have realized that an employee was … our expansion by providing proprietary information to a competitor.
   a damaging **b** injuring **c** undermining **d** weakening
8 Because the staff questionnaire deals with a sensitive topic, we have to consider how best to … responses from all employees.
   a elicit **b** provoke **c** solve **d** unlock
9 He told … he was being bullied by a colleague on a daily basis.
   a that **b** to us **c** to us that **d** us that
10 All things …, permitting employees to telework part of the week increases job satisfaction.
   a considered **b** in all **c** put together **d** taken together

11. Most employees take advantage of the generous ... benefits offered here.
    a extra service b fringe c perk d pony
12. Considering your ability to help build consensus, you are ... an asset to the company.
    a clearly b particularly c rather d thoroughly

Dealing with legal matters   Points

13. ... our client, we hereby inform you that you are infringing upon our client's trademark.
    a In the name of b On behalf of c Representing
    d Under contract of
14. No sooner had they received the letter ... they called to set an appointment.
    a had b than c then d when
15. In regard to our response to the cease and desist letter, do you think we should play for ... and see what happens?
    a fun b keeps c time d wins
16. The website ... that the company illegally collected client data over a period of five years.
    a accuses b alleges c condones d endorses

Compliance & the public   Points

17. The public ... against the unethical behaviour of the CEO resulted in his immediate replacement.
    a backlash b backslash c endorsement d response
18. During the press conference, the CEO pledged to ... all known details to the public.
    a disclose b publicize c recognize d uncover
19. Matters of safety are of ... importance to us.
    a biggest b equal c most d utmost
20. We of course expect our subcontractors to ... safety and ethical standards.
    a assure b hold up c keep d uphold

Total points: / 20

Answer key

Unit 1 pages 5–10

1 Individual answers.

2
1. A Have you processed, B 've (have) been working
2. A 's (has) worked / 's (has) been working
3. A 've (have) conducted
4. A 've (have) been negotiating, 've (have) only closed
5. A Have you drafted / been drafting
   B have been waiting

3
1. … and see how much households and individuals actually spend …: Here "actually" is used to emphasize "spend" and to point out that they were looking to uncover the truth about the amounts spent. An English synonym could be "in reality"; the German translation is *wirklich*.
2. … actual consumers …: Similar to Ex. 1, "actual" is used in the sense of "true" or "real"; the German translation is *echt*.
3. Well, you know, actually, …: "Actually" is often used in response to questions in order to make both positive and negative responses more polite (so that the person who posed the question does not appear unintelligent), in the sense of the German *eigentlich*.
4. It was, actually: In this case, the speaker is using "actually" to emphasize a surprising detail in an answer, in the sense of the German *tatsächlich*.

4 **1** c, **2** f, **3** d, **4** a, **5** e, **6** b

5 **Questions that check information during introductions:**
Am I saying that correctly? / And you're Anna Hattig? / And is it Benjamin or Ben? / We were just wondering if we could use first names, I mean, all of us …

Phrases or sentences that put forward ideas or requests:
Well, I don't know if it's possible, but I was thinking that … / That is, if you have the time. / I was thinking we might be able to … / I was hoping to hear more …

Phrases or sentences that express empathy or interest:
Well, since I'm new, I imagine all of you must be very curious … / That sounds really exciting. / It must be quite a challenge.

Statements that express knowledge about someone's experience:
So, Jörg, I hear you're the creative head of packaging. / You must be very proud of your many patents.

6 **1** b, **2** a
1. managed to reach
2. managed to win
3. managed / managed to move
4. managed
5. managed

7 *Example (Anna):*
Exactly what do you propose? = I was wondering exactly what you had in mind.
How about next week? = I was thinking (that) next week might be good.
I think two days would be best. = Perhaps we could set something up for two days?
An answer today would be great. = I was hoping you could send an answer today. Do you think that would be possible?

Example (Azra):
If that's feasible, of course. = Of course that depends on your schedule as well.
I'm not sure. = Sorry, I can't say at the moment. I'll have to get back to you.
I'll have to check and let you know. = I understand that two days would be optimal for you. I still need to check with my colleagues.
I'll do my best. = I'll be in touch as soon as possible.

8 *Example:*
That is a very complex process. Would you mind telling me more about ...?
I'm terribly sorry, but I didn't completely catch that. Could you go over it again for me if it's not too much trouble?

9 Individual answers.

10 **2** on, **3** to/with, **4** to, **5** on/with, **6** on/with, **7** on

Unit 2 pages 11–16

1

Noun	Verb	Adjective
validation	to validate	validated/valid
confirmation	to confirm	confirmed
notification	to notify	notified
remittance	to remit	remitted
shipment	to ship	shipped

2 **1** effect, verb: to bring about; to cause something to happen
2 affect, verb: to impact on something; to have an effect on something
3 effect, noun: an impact; a change that is due to an action or other cause

3 Individual answers.

4 **1** d, **2** a, **3** c, **4** b
Individual answers.

5 *Example:*
Introduction – states the key information about the topic and report; gives an overview of what will be discussed and the aim of the report; simple present
Description – provides detailed information, including dates, times, changes, problems, successes, etc.; simple past, active and passive voice
Conclusion – sums up the information in the description section; looks at all the data together and analyzes their meaning or importance; simple past
Recommendations – gives suggestions about how to proceed and/or to prevent additional problems in the future; in some reports it also suggests a decision; future/conditionals, active voice

6 **a** If, **b** f
Individual answers.

7 Verb, Synonym, Collocation
to come together, to work out, a project comes / things come together
to simulate, to create a model or representation of, to simulate the plans
to pose, to put forward, to pose a risk / to pose a problem
to clear, to officially approve, to clear a plan
to fine-tune, to make small adjustments, to fine-tune the simulations

8 We were unaware of the problem until week 20, when we were more than halfway through the project. It first came to our attention when the client examined a prototype and then claimed that we weren't meeting the specifications according to the contract. The issue was that they had changed their requirements, but only informed one engineer who left our company for another job only two weeks later. We didn't anticipate any difficulty to arise at that late stage, so we had allowed much of our staff to go on scheduled leave. How did we deal with the situation? We outsourced it to specialists. To avoid the dilemma in the future, I suggest that the specification version is always stated in the contract, and that we always do a final check of the specifications with the client before we begin any engineering. In the end, it has cost us both time and money, and has damaged the relationship with a long-standing client.

9 *Example:*
The graph shows the sales of our product XY in the year Z. The horizontal axis shows the months, and the vertical axis depicts sales in [e.g.] thousands of euros. Following a steady rise from January until March, sales dropped dramatically in April. They rose steadily until July but stagnated throughout August, September and October. Then the figures jumped to a new peak.

10 a) *Please see transcript no. 43 on pages 67 and 68 and/or listen to track 43 on the CD.*
  b) a very exciting event: a nail biter
  the depth of the situation: the big picture
  to have a heavy workload to manage: to have a lot on one's plate
  c) Right. I had heard there would be some changes.
  Sounds like he's off to a good start.
  He's got a lot on his plate, hasn't he?

11 *Example:*
  1 Although the buyers made many recommendations for improvement, the company did not update its system. As a result, sales were negatively affected.
  2 The claims that proprietary information was being passed on by our preferred supplier were made by a competitor. Once it had become clear that the claims were unsubstantiated, the competitor withdrew its bid.

Unit 3 pages 17–23

1 **1** d, **2** e, **3** b, **4** a, **5** c / **1** pleased about, hammer out: **2** partner in, follow up on: **3** contributed to

2 **1** … would be providing about ten hours a week of communication-related activities and reporting to Yves and Bill. / conditional continuous to describe a tentative action
  2 … will be helping out Bill and Yves. / future continuous to describe what will be in progress in the future
  3 … are meeting with Zara. / present continuous to describe concrete arrangements
  4 … will be working with Bill and Yves's department. / future continuous to describe what will be in progress in the future
  5 … will be working with multiple departments. / future continuous to describe what will be in progress in the future
  6 … are showing Zara around the company. / present continuous to describe concrete arrangements
  7 … will talk with her about the aims of the project and the tasks they'll be counting on her to handle. / future continuous to describe what will be in progress in the future

3 **1** c, **2** a, **3** d, **4** e, **5** b, **6** f
  a to confirm information already stated: 1, 6
  b to request clarification on a point: 2, 4
  c to respond by giving a suggestion or a contrast: 3, 5

  Example:
  1 Before we go any further, let me make sure I've understood you correctly. / If I understand you correctly, you simply decided not to follow the company's standard procedure?
  2 Can you spell out the four sub-tasks for me? / Could you explain each of the sub-tasks to me step by step?
  3 Before we go any further, let me make sure I've understood – you now expect that the project will be four weeks late? / If I understand you correctly, the project is going to be four weeks late?
  4 Could you explain to me why the team – now with an additional team member – can't handle the project's scope? / Can you spell out exactly what this means?

4 *Example:*
  1 The following Proposal for Services is based on the information provided by Ellen Wagner of Schulze Automotive Holding GmbH & Co. KG during a phone call on November 13, 20xx as well as the RFP dated November 14, 20xx.
  2 The client shall provide the contractor all documentation required for the investigation without undue delay.
  3 Up to 20 % of the total bill (including VAT) will be billed for incidental expenses incurred during project-related travel.
  4 Disclosure of the final project report or the project results to third parties, including any reproductions and translations into foreign languages, is not permitted without the express written consent of Energy Consulting Ltd.

5
1 be on the same page
2 ballpark figure; bottom line
3 the pinch
4 a participant; a benchmark

6 *Example:*
A: Thank you for holding/waiting. How may I/can I help you?
B: Am I speaking to Nicole O'Reilly?
A: Yes, this is Nicole.
B: Hello, Ms O'Reilly, this is Thomas Olbermann from Olbermann International. I'm calling with regard to / about a potential project. I got your name from Olivia Gomez. I understand / have learned / was told that your team did / conducted / carried out some research for her company last year. Are you the correct/right person to speak to about an upcoming project?
A: Yes, I'm the team leader/manager.
B: Great. Well, we're a small German talent recruitment agency and we're considering / thinking about / discussing the possibility of expansion into the Eastern European market. We'd like for you to research the recruitment market in regard to our niche – engineers within the energy industry.
A: That's definitely/certainly something we can help you with. What we would need from you is an RFP / a description of the work you'd like to have carried out.
B: We're sending them out / distributing it today, so it should reach you shortly. Our company policy requires that we solicit/request three separate bids before making/reaching a decision. In the meantime, would you be willing/able to send us some information about the key research services you provide as well as some client references? Olivia told me about the work you carried out / completed / did for her company – they were very happy/pleased/satisfied, so we already know of one satisfied / pleased / happy customer.
A: Yes, of course, I'd be happy to.

B: One more question: assuming we decide/decided to work with you, when can you / could you / would it be possible for you to begin? What we don't want is for a competitor to enter the market even weeks ahead of us.
A: I'm afraid / I'm sorry / Unfortunately, I can't answer that until I see the RFP and gain a better understanding of the project's scope/requirements/depth.
B: Of course. I understand. You can expect the RFP later today via email. Thanks very much for your time.

7 *Example:*
RFP 43-2013
Olbermann International is a small German talent recruitment agency. Since 2008 we've supported engineering professionals and engineering firms specialized in the energy industry. Matching sharp minds to outstanding professional opportunities – that's what we're known for.
Due to our success as well as the growing need for energy companies to work with cross-border interests in mind, we would now like to explore the possibility of expanding our services into neighbouring countries, namely Poland, the Czech Republic, Hungary, and Slovakia.
We would like the successful contractor to
1 research the respective markets in regard to current talent recruitment agencies,
2 research the respective markets to explore how many multilingual engineering professionals are currently active, and
3 research the educational programme equivalents to Dipl.-Ing. offered at institutions of higher education in the above-mentioned countries, as well as the number of multilingual graduates per year. This research and its concluding report should be completed no later than April 30, 20XX.
Please provide a bid no later than 5 pm on February 28, 20XX. We are only able to accept bids submitted via email or fax. Our decision will be communicated no later than March 5, 20XX.

8 *Example:*
Knowledge management ensures that what people know about their jobs, for example how tasks and their jobs are carried out over the course of an entire project, is shared among colleagues within an organization. Scrum methods facilitate knowledge exchange by means of formal and informal communication opportunities as well as post-project meetings, from which modifications to processes and templates can be made.

9 1 to cultivate   5 to confront
    2 to draft   6 constant
    3 constrained   7 to compile
    4 concentrated   8 indispensable

Individual answers.

10 1 a, 2 c, 3 a, 4 a, 5 b, 6 a, 7 c

Example:
In the first sentence of each set, the adjectives are placed at the end of the sentence (in the predicate) following a form of *to be*. However, those words become compound modifiers when they are positioned directly before the noun and, because both words are vital and work together to modify the noun, they are joined by a hyphen, as together they are considered one unit.

Unit 4 pages 24-29

1 1 suggestion, **2** idea, **3** issue, **4** process, **5** decision

2 Individual answers.

3 *Example:*
  1 Sorry, Maria, Serena, can we just let Raymond finish please? / Hold on a minute. Let's let Raymond complete his thoughts first. / Let's try to speak one at a time – these conference calls are always tough since we can't see each other. It seems to me that Raymond had some information to add.
  2 Please, speaking about the situation in this aggressive manner is not going to get us anywhere. Let's deal with the order and then we can explore how to improve communication among team members in the future. Okay? Now, let's look at … / Hold on. Let's see what we can do to improve the situation with the order, and then we can talk about future internal communication.
  3 I understand you're both busy, but the Sanders project clearly needs to be handled by one of you. One alternative is to split the tasks between you. How does that sound? / I know there's a lot going on right now, but in the end this project has to be handled by one of you. How do you suggest we work this out?

4 1 j, **2** a, **3** d, **4** i, **5** g, **6** e, **7** f, **8** c, **9** b, **10** h

1 2, 6 / **2** 4, 9 / **3** 5, 8 / **4** 3, 7 / **5** 1, 10

5 I noticed that … / Next time, could you …? / It would be helpful if … / It doesn't seem that … / I would appreciate it if … / Could you …?
Polite phrases: I, could, would, it
less polite phrases: you, need, should, can't

6 *Example:*
  1 Just until you gain more experience, could you let me or one of the more experienced colleagues talk with the clients?
  2 Next time, could you consult with me prior to making any decisions?
  3 It doesn't seem that the email was attached. Could you please resend it with the attachment?
  4 It would be helpful if you notified me whenever the Wi-Fi goes down. Every minute is valuable!
  5 I noticed that you sent the confirmation without approval from production. Please avoid doing that in the future since it could result in both an unfulfilled order and a dissatisfied customer.
  6 I'd appreciate it if in the future you could clearly state exactly what you need us to do so that we can make sure that everything's on track.

7 *Example:*
 1 A: frustrating / irritating / infuriating
   B: guess / can understand that / can see that / can imagine
 2 A: take care of / finalize / finish / work out
   B: frustrated / irritated / angry
 3 A: guessing what's going to happen / shooting in the dark / jumping to conclusions / guessing the details
   B: like to know / be happy to receive / welcome / be grateful for

8 1 There's no need to put him on the spot.
 2 It would be best if the two of you talked it over.
 3 I guess I may have misinterpreted your message.
 4 It seems like we've gotten off on the wrong foot.

9 *Example:*
Might you have a minute to run through the figures? It's rather urgent.
Do you think you could give Francine a call and see if she has time on Tuesday?
It looks like that decision will have negative consequences for us.
Thanks for stopping by. Do you think we could connect later? I have a three o'clock deadline.

10 1 false: linguist, **2** true, **3** true, **4** false: Germans, **5** true

Unit 5 pages 30-35

1 *Example:*
TrinkO was selling products successfully in German-speaking countries when it started selling in Poland and the Czech Republic.
As TrinkO was developing a new sports drink, they had a product breakthrough.
Between 2008 and 2012 TrinkO was looking for partnering firms in Western Europe; during that time the company was approached by a potential partner in South America.
They had established key contacts in Asia and started selling in Japan and Vietnam before they redirected their efforts to South America.
TrinkO had started selling in Eastern Europe before it searched for partnering distributors elsewhere.

2 1 production / output / net income / earnings / earnings per share / prices / investment / operating result / sales
 2 net income / earnings / earning per share / production / output / investment / operating result / sales
 3 operating result / net income / earnings / sales

3 *Example:*
Sales rose by roughly 3.5 billion euros over the previous year.
Earnings increased by just under 1 billion euros over the previous year.
Between last year and this year, the share price dropped by roughly 8 % / by just under 8 %.

4 *Example:*
 1 (If I had accepted that job in Scotland,) I would have a lot more responsibility than I do today.
 2 (If I had noticed it before the audit,) I would have alerted the CFO immediately.
 3 Would we have been able to invest in new assets such as the new building and the equipment if we hadn't applied for and received the government subsidy?
 4 What would the composition of our workforce look like today if we hadn't been committed to promoting social equity?
 5 No, they wouldn't be significantly higher (if we had licensed out production).
 6 Yes, we probably would have been able to raise enough private capital (if we hadn't gone public in 2012).

5 1 downsize, **2** liquidate, **3** high places, **4** the bottom fell out, **5** trailblazer, **6** undermine, **7** pioneer. Solution: SUSTAIN

6 *Example:*
the history of the problem, the expected results – quantifiable or qualifiable, specifications, deadlines, contact person, budget

7 We've invited you here today in order to …
So, just to get you up to speed: …
Without going into too much detail, …
That being said, however, …
It's a recognized fact that …
We need to take steps …
In sum, what we'd like to do now is …
In other words, …
We'll provide you …
Do you think you could prepare a proposal for the study, concretely outlining the methodology, within a week?
… would also be helpful.

8 Individual answers.

9 *Example:*
The client operates two gas-fired power plants and one coal-fired plant which provide power to the region as well as two industrial plants. To support the client in exploring the feasibility of replacing at least half of the energy produced by the coal-fired plant with renewable energy sources, a feasibility study was carried out. The aim of the feasibility study was to assess and update the findings of a previous study carried out in 2007. The time periods to be considered were 10, 20, and 50 years, taking into account both partial and full replacement of the coal-fired plant with photovoltaic or wind plants. The findings showed that the investment costs of a partial replacement would be recovered within 10 years, and the costs of a full replacement would be recovered within 22 years after making the initial financial investment without relying on government subsidies.

10 *Example:*
– 2012 was successful, but not due to noteworthy financial results
– decisive events: advances in the development of programmes in the clinical pipeline
– response was a share price increase, the re-rating of the company by investors
– response illustrates that investors link value to the building momentum and progress in the pipeline rather than financial results

11 1 If we had raised more capital, we would have been able to expand our overseas operations.
2 We should have taken more steps to improve our sustainability.
3 Sorry, I didn't make myself clear.
4 We're very happy with what we've seen so far.
5 I understand your concern.
6 I'm glad you brought it up.

Unit 6 pages 36–42

1 1 There are a lot of positive things to say about, The downside is **2** On the one hand, On the other hand **3** To me, the biggest perk is **4** On the whole / Overall, **5** Overall / On the whole, has made a big difference

2 To give your own view: personally, from my perspective, as I see it
To restate an idea: in other words, said differently, to put it another way
To look at the big picture: all things considered, taking every aspect into account, if we take a step back, we can see that
To state the information you know about a situation: I am aware, I've been told, my understanding is

3 1 whether I had asked Doris about next year's training opportunities.
2 (that) I talk with Carla about it.
3 that we / they would announce the pay cuts soon.
4 were born, she had been having / has been having difficulty managing her work-life balance. (2 possible answers)
5 he is / was sorry and that he isn't / wasn't able to volunteer on Saturdays due to family commitments. (2 possible answers) he is / was only available in the evenings.
6 that she was going to change jobs in December.

4 1 that she would have / had her performance evaluation the next day / on Wednesday.
2 that she had successfully closed a deal with a new client the day before / the previous day / on Monday.

3 that last week they had / had had a meeting with the team leader who will be filling in for Carla while she's on maternity leave.
4 that their / his company had adopted a generous long-service bonus policy the year before / the previous year.
5 that he would attend a trade fair in Barcelona two months from then / in February / this month.
6 that he would take two weeks' holiday this month.

5 1 E/b, 2 A/a, 3 A/d, 4 E/c

6 Example:
2 I agree. 3 Honestly, I'm very surprised to hear that. 4 I'm happy to hear that.

7 See transcript on page 71.

8 Example:
She said that they have been / had been particularly impressed by how well I've / I had adapted to working as part of the international team. She told me that the client for which I led a project has / had approached them about future collaboration as well.

9 Example:
1 "What kinds of steps have you taken?"
2 "Where do you think the difficulty seems to lie?"
3 "Could you describe some of the tasks you've been assigned and some of the tasks you had expected to receive?"
4 "What kinds of programmes are you interested in taking part in?"

10 Example:
1 to use a specific process to measure or evaluate something
2 to find common ground between two diverse aims
3 to be deeply involved in social and professional connections within a company or organization
4 to measure someone according to the expectation for the field or profession
5 to evaluate by how much
6 to have extreme interest in something; due to your strong interest, it spreads to others

7 the amount to which one thing matches another

11 Individual answers.

12 1 Despite my efforts to keep the lines of communication open, I started to feel out of the loop.
2 It will take much longer than you expect – the process is full of red tape.
3 I heard that a team member said I wasn't pulling my weight.
4 There was clearly a communication breakdown while he was teleworking.
5 We need to assess the degree to which annual appraisals improve performance.

Unit 7 pages 43-48

1 a 4, 8; b 1, 6; c 2, 5; d 3, 7

2 1 B We would only offer discounts to our key clients. / We used to only offer discounts to our key clients.
2 S Compliance used to be extremely vague and never monitored.
3 B We wouldn't hire service dealers. / We didn't use to hire service dealers.
4 B Before we extended our warranty, some customers would call every week to complain. / Before we extended our warranty, some customers used to call every week to complain.
5 S We used to have a complicated price structure.

3 General changes: relative clauses were reduced; relative clauses were converted to adjective-noun structures

1 On-site testing is optimal for testing new equipment.
2 Compliance certification requires a long process.
3 Companies promoting sustainability achieve better market results.
4 Contacts made at the speed networking event resulted in new clients.

4 See transcript on page 72.

5 1 She addresses supply and demand, competition and quality.
2 Product: an exclusive feature is mentioned, although it's not named; the product has been recognized as having both clinical and technical quality
Price: the question the speaker poses is whether or not the price should be raised; it's implied that quantity discounts are offered
Place: not mentioned
Promotion: focus promotion on the additional feature; the possibility of using the device for cross-selling
3 She says that several people contacted her upon receiving the agenda.
She says that it's necessary to reach consensus.
She opens the floor to questions as soon as she's made her case.
4 food for thought / more bang for one's buck / to hear something through the grapevine

6 claimed / cease / contested / won / cease / withdrawn / filed / scare

7 1 Not only did they unveil a nearly identical product, they also gave it a similar name.
2 No sooner had they filed the trademark application than we received a letter from their lawyer.
3 Under no circumstances should you acknowledge responsibility.
4 Never before have such high monetary damages been awarded.
5 Only rarely do SMEs stand their ground against industry giants.
6 In no way does our use of the image infringe the copyright.

8 *Example:*
Paragraph 4: Since Nutella is a registered trademark, we always look into how and why the Nutella name is being used by people outside of the company. For this reason, the Nutella brand name on the fan page caught our attention. In sum, we wanted to make sure that the way the trademark was being used was aligned with our corporate guidelines.

Paragraph 8: It's unclear to me why a cease and desist letter was sent to Sara Rosso. It seems that she has only helped to promote your product.
Paragraph 9: A nice promotion for Ms Rosso would have probably been a better response. She is, after all, a big Nutella fan. Plus, isn't it in your best interest for customers to buy your product?
Last paragraph: Ferrero is happy to have devoted and loyal fans of Nutella, such as Sara Rosso.

9 Individual answers.

10 1 Cutting corners leads to higher risk.
2 Ralf is a conscientious employee who has been instrumental in ensuring data security for users of our mobile app.
3 No sooner had we sent the cease and desist letter than we received calls from the media.
4 Under no circumstances should you respond without consulting with our lawyer.
5 We hereby confirm receipt of your letter dated April 19.
6 Unforeseen circumstances prevented us from responding within the timeframe requested.

Unit 8 pages 49-53

1 Individual answers.

2 2 The facts currently known about the situation – one of their suppliers has been subcontracting to sweatshops
3 The company's reaction to the known facts – they do not condone this
4 Promises regarding how the situation will be handled – they will investigate
5 Steps that will be taken in the immediate future – creating an accord on workplace monitoring and HR management

3 Individual answers.

4 to condemn: to express absolute disapproval of
to condone: to officially approve

to disclose: to make information known that is either new or had been secret
to exert: to apply something
to field: to deal with
to flag: to mark something in order to draw attention to it
to pledge: to promise

1 fielding/pledged, **2** condone/condemn, **3** exerted/disclose/flagged

5 infinitive: promise, intend, fail, claim, seem; gerund: discuss, imagine, appreciate, consider, suggest; either infinitive or gerund: regret, stop, forget, remember, try

Example:
Verb: to remember
1 Infinitive: I didn't remember to pick up the mail.
  Meaning: I did not complete the task.
2 Gerund: I don't remember picking up the mail.
  Meaning: I completed the task, but do not remember doing the activity.

6 from the audio: by this I mean …
additional examples: in other words, for example, what I mean by xyz is, that includes, more specifically, namely

7 1 I would say that turnover is most closely linked to customer satisfaction.
2 It helps to some extent if it is part of a larger reporting and PR strategy.
3 On the whole, we need to make the supply chain more visible.
4 By and large, it will appear as if the manufacturer has something to hide.
5 For all practical purposes, they do tend to help to some degree.

a 2, **b** 4, **c** 5, **d** 1, **e** 3

8 Individual answers.

Additional information for subsequent paragraphs:
A quote or two from a key player or key players – who should be quoted and what details should it include?
Background information
Acknowledgement of programme partners

9 1 formal, professional, 2 complete sentences using correct grammar, 3 mostly full words 4 accomplishments or positive messages from the company; the tweets do not respond to or address criticism or negative situations

10 Individual answers.

11 1 We were shocked and deeply saddened to learn of the unsafe working conditions at the factory which resulted in the deaths of two workers.
2 We will do our utmost to rectify the situation immediately.
3 The approach appears to be feasible, however we are concerned about the real outcome.
4 Well, it is a solution of sorts.
5 DYK decreasing your environmental footprint can save your company thousands each year? Join our live chat with experts Tuesday at 9 am. #footprint

Progress Check 1 Unit 1-4

Describing your work & dealing with colleagues
1 c, **2** d, **3** b, **4** b, **5** d

Projects & processes
6 b, **7** b, **8** d, **9** a, **10** c, **11** d

Discussing possibilities
12 b, **13** b, **14** c, **15** c

Internal communication
16 a, **17** a, **18** d, **19** c, **20** c

Progress Check 2 Unit 5-8

Business decisions & results
1 a, **2** a, **3** c, **4** b, **5** d, **6** b

Managing personnel
7 c, **8** a, **9** d, **10** a, **11** b, **12** a

Dealing with legal matters
13 b, **14** b, **15** c, **16** b

Compliance & the public
17 a, **18** a, **19** d, **20** d

Transcripts

Unit 1

 Exercise 7

An = Anna, Az = Azra
Az: Hello, Anna.
An: Hi Azra, good to see you! I'm sorry we didn't get a chance to talk much following the meeting. I wanted to check in with you about your idea for me to shadow each department. Exactly what do you propose?
Az: Well, it depends on what you'd like to do, Anna. I mean, we would be happy to have you in the department for a day or two. If that's feasible, of course.
An: That would be fantastic! I'll start the shadowing in your department. Since I'm just getting started with the project, my schedule is fairly open. How about next week?
Az: I'm not sure. I mean, we'd be happy to have you, but I have to check the schedule and confirm the plans with my colleagues. We have some compliance audits coming up.
An: Sure. I think two days would be best.
Az: I'll have to check and let you know.
An: Okay, I'll look for your message. An answer today would be great. I have to set my schedule for next week.
Az: I'll do my best.
An: Thanks!

Unit 2

 Exercise 10

J = Jarrett, W = Werner
J: Hello Werner, great game last night, wasn't it?
W: Yeah, hard to believe that our team scored the winning goal in the last minute.
J: I know! It was a nail biter, wasn't it? So, Werner, I was out yesterday, home because my son was sick, so I didn't get to attend the big meeting. Could you give me a quick overview?
W: Sure, Jarrett, no problem. Well, first of all, it looks like we need to invest in improvements to our operations due to new legislation as well as market pressure. The root of both of these is deregulation.
J: Right. I had heard there would be some changes.
W: Exactly. To make sure that the investments are worthwhile, they're looking at the big picture and taking a holistic approach. They've made some simple changes that have resulted in significant increases to efficiency. Three examples he gave were changes to locomotive inspections, reductions in excess inventory, and the optimization of our car type portfolio.
J: Sounds like he's off to a good start.
W: Absolutely. And no surprise, ERP plays a key role. So, the next step will be coordinating the rolling stock maintenance. For that we'll need to create and implement a new inventory module that can be used by people all over Europe. It actually looks like the toughest part will be getting people to use the module once it's out there.
J: He's got a lot on his plate, hasn't he?
W: Yes, definitely.
J: You know what I'd like to suggest to him? I'd suggest installing some sort of incentive to motivate the system users to enter info into the system.

W: Yes, he said this means that the information needs to be available to the users in the local languages, not just German or English.
J: Oh, sure, that's a good point, but if there were football tickets given as prizes for the person who inputs the most data each week or each month, for example – now that would be an idea that would motivate everyone!
W: Right, Jarrett, why don't you suggest that to Mr. Galdiks?

Unit 3

Exercise 3
E = Ellen, Y = Yves
E: Hello, Yves? It's Ellen. How were your holidays?
Y: Fine thanks, how about yours?
E: Very nice, thank you. Say, Yves, before the holidays we spoke briefly about your project portfolio in general and the MDM project in particular.
Y: Right.
E: And thanks for sending along the job description, especially fitting it in before the holidays. Now, if I understood the description correctly, the student trainee would be providing about ten hours a week of communication-related activities.
Y: That's right.
E: And who would she be reporting to? The job description just says "Green IT Management Team." So she'd be working closely with you and Bill?
Y: That's right. At this point we haven't completely decided who would be doing what. What do you think is the likelihood that she'll be helping us out in the coming months?
E: Oh, it's definitely a "go". I just needed to confirm those details regarding the job description. The student trainee – her name is Zara Späth – has just arrived for her traineeship and we're meeting with her tomorrow to talk about her responsibilities while she's here. So by this time next week she'll be working with you and your team. You can even expect her to put in a full 40 hours by the end of the month. She'll be supporting multiple departments on a weekly basis, so it's important that we synchronize her schedule carefully. How does two hours a day from nine till 11 each morning sound?
Y: Sounds perfect.
E: Will you be needing us to provide a workspace for her?
Y: No, we have a desk that's free at the moment.
E: OK. We're showing her around the company on Wednesday. How about we bring her to your office at nine to introduce her?
Y: That's fine. I'll ask Bill to come by and we can talk with her a little bit about the aims of the project and the tasks we'll be counting on her to handle while she's on board.

Unit 4

Exercise 4
R = Raymond, M = Maria, S = Serena
R: Sure, I'd be happy to. We've researched several container sizes and have found that the largest size, while the cheapest, actually poses a long-term dilemma for us due to its overall incompatibility with the internal parameters of our warehouse. Frankly, we wouldn't be able to maneuver the units easily within the warehouse, so ...
M: What do you mean you wouldn't be able to maneuver them easily? Isn't it possible to reconfigure the setup of the warehouse to accommodate them?
S: Ray, according to the email you sent yesterday, considering the budget that's the only size that is feasible for us.

46 V = Vic, T = Terry
V: Well, unfortunately, we've run into yet another communication problem with the Maritime and Hydrographic Agency. As a result, we've had to reroute our inland water shipments using rail. Not only does this eat away at the profit on the order, it also puts any future orders with the company at risk. We might have avoided this situation if you had kept the team better informed, Terry.
T: You can see the internal schedule just as easily as anyone else, Vic. My holiday time had been clearly marked for months, and if you look at the meeting minutes from last month's telecon, you can see that this point was specifically addressed. It was up to you to liaise with the Agency.

47 R = Robin, M = Mel
R: Sorry, I just haven't got the time to take on another project. I'm already working till at least seven every night – one of our team members has been out because his child's ill. Due to the severity of the illness, it appears that I'll be covering for him for the foreseeable future.
M: I would love to help you out, but my priority is dealing with the faulty pallets that have come in from the US. If we don't solve that issue, we'll be unable to pack and ship our goods efficiently and the knock-on effect will be delays to the bulk of our orders.

Unit 5

48 Exercise 7
We've invited you here today in order to give you some insight into a feasibility study that we'd like to have carried out and to see if you might be interested in putting together a proposal for it. So, just to get you up to speed: We operate two gas-fired power plants and one coal-fired plant. Without going into too much detail, they provide electricity to the region as well as to two industrial plants – a car manufacturer and a steel refinery.
Thanks to changes overseas, coal has become extremely inexpensive and so we've had little financial motivation to change our means of production.
That being said, however, we are committed to becoming an active participant in the energy transition to renewable energy sources. We envisage replacing at least half, if not all, of the energy produced by our coal-fired plant with renewable energy sources.
We had conducted a preliminary study in 2007, but subsequently decided against the investment – despite the government subsidies that were available. It's a recognized fact that our board tends to err on the side of caution, especially where new technologies are concerned. But now the pressure within the industry has increased and we need to take steps to improve our reputation as an energy provider that is sustainable in both senses of the word.
In sum, what we'd like to do now is commission a feasibility study that assesses and updates the findings of the 2007 study and specifically focuses on financial projections for the next 10, 20, and 50 years if we replaced our coal-fired plant with either photovoltaic or wind plants. In other words, both variants should be explored. We'll provide you a summary of the results from the 2007 study, but we're unable to simply copy the full study due to the terms of our contract with the consulting firm. If I – oh, yes, I would be your contact person in this case – but if I forwarded those results to you by tomorrow at the latest, do you think you could prepare a proposal for the study, concretely outlining the methodology, within a week? Several references would also be helpful.

Unit 6

49 Exercise 7

R = HR representative, E = employee

R: We've been particularly impressed by how well you've adapted to working as part of our international team. We know it's never easy to start fresh in a new city, or country in your case. Several members of the supervisory team have complimented you on your performance. Particularly the project with TRIAD was mentioned – I believe that was the first project you oversaw from start to finish? It says here you have "the unique ability to make sure that everyone's ideas are heard and respected, even those coming from the more junior members of the team. This ability has fostered a true sense of team spirit. All phases progressed smoothly and the client has already approached us about future collaborations, provided that the projects have the same team leader."

50 E: Well, first let me say how much I appreciate that feedback. You're definitely correct – starting a new job in a different country has had its challenging moments. I'm very happy to know that the way I've organized and managed the team has been successful and recognized. Of course there are minor changes I would make in the future, but overall I was also pleased with how we carried out the project.

51 R: That takes us to our next point: initiating action. I'm reluctant to say that there's been some disappointment, because overall your work is satisfactory. However, there has been some doubt about whether you are actually working up to your full potential. We just spoke about a very successful project that you managed, but we feel that there has been a lack of interest on your part in taking on additional complex projects.

52 E: I'm a bit surprised to hear that. I took on the TRIAD project because I was specifically asked to do so. I wasn't aware that I had the opportunity to volunteer – rather, my feeling was that projects are generally assigned. Apparently that was an oversight on my part. I do admit that there have been several projects I would have been interested in overseeing, but I had the feeling that the senior team members generally are given priority. If that's not the case, I guess I need to take more initiative in the future.

53 R: That sounds like a good plan. Let's proceed to our final category: technical skills. It looks as if this is your weakest point. We are a little concerned that your efficiency – while overall quite good – suffers due to the difficulty you have navigating the software programs, particularly our proprietary software. Do you agree?

54 E: Hmmm. That takes me a bit by surprise. I might need some time to think of an appropriate response. … It is true that I've prioritized managing my daily work – including the TRIAD project – and subsequently may have overlooked the need to become fully competent with the internal system. Whenever I've had trouble, which I suppose is about once or twice a week, I've simply asked a colleague for help and never gave it a second thought that I wasn't developing the skills required to adequately handle the software on my own.

But I do see what you mean. Relying on my colleagues' assistance could be annoying on their side, not to mention that it interrupts their work and thus reduces their efficiency. Do you think it might be possible to attend some sort of internal training so that I can improve my skills?

Unit 7

 55 **Exercise 4**

The final part of our annual product performance evaluation for the TPX 5000 concerns the price. Upon receiving the meeting agenda, several of you even contacted me in advance regarding this point.
To get right to the point: The disinfection device has been so successful in the market that we're considering raising the price. We know that this would be a rather unusual step, but we feel confident that it's the right decision for reasons we'd like to outline now.
First, we have the question of supply and demand. Demand has far exceeded our expectations, and we haven't been able to produce enough units to fill the orders within the time frames requested by our clients. Production has reached full capacity, and short of building a new factory, we are unable to increase our production rate. Based on the basic law of supply and demand, we could raise our prices by at least 15 per cent.
Now, second is the question of competition. We used to be the only manufacturer that provided such a device. Since we entered the market in 2012, three competitors have launched similar devices. Their prices are roughly the same as ours, but we have heard through the grapevine that our competitors generally do not offer quantity discounts.

Third is a matter of quality. From a clinical and technical perspective, our device performs better than those of our competitors and has an additional feature that our competitors' devices don't. If we were to thus differentiate our product within the market by focusing on this feature, we could certainly justify to the clients that they are getting more bang for their buck.
For these three reasons, which we can back up with financial and statistical evidence, we feel that raising our price by five to ten per cent is indeed justified. But we need consensus on this. Our market position is stable and as we launch additional devices, we intend to use our firm position with the TPX 5000 as a basis for cross-selling.
OK, now that I've given you some food for thought, I'm eager to hear your questions.

Unit 8

 56 **Exercise 6**

Classical compliance, and by this I mean adhering to standards, regulations, and other requirements, is an approach that provides a solution of sorts. It can provide certain assurances, but the overall effort does not seem to be aligned with the industry. The whole approach would appear to be a bit short-sighted. I would say, for all practical purposes, the only real outcome is illegal subcontracting, with all its adverse social and environmental impacts.